# Zapotec Civilization

*A Captivating Guide to the Pre-Columbian Cloud People Who Dominated the Valley of Oaxaca in Mesoamerica*

# Free Bonus from Captivating History (Available for a Limited time)

Hi History Lovers!

Now you have a chance to join our exclusive history list so you can get your first history ebook for free as well as discounts and a potential to get more history books for free! Simply visit the link below to join.

Captivatinghistory.com/ebook

Also, make sure to follow us on:

Twitter: @Captivhistory

Facebook: Captivating History:@captivatinghistory

# Contents

# Introduction

When people discuss the civilizations encountered by the Conquistadors as they traveled across South America and Mesoamerica, they will always bring up the Incans, Mayans, and Aztecs. These civilizations had large pyramids and structured societies that the Conquistadors studied, and history has assigned them a pivotal role in growth and development during the Pre-Columbian times. However, they were not the only civilizations.

Less well-known are the Zapotec. Even though they are obscure today, they lived and thrived, and became a civilization of interest to the Conquistadors. They did not leave behind the same kinds of massive structures and temples like other civilizations, so they have not left behind much for those people interested in learning about their culture. Historians have a wealth of details about these influential people through the writings of the Conquistadors. The journals and letters show how intensely interested the Europeans were in trying to understand the civilization and its complex system and relationships. While much of what is known today comes from these biased journals, archaeologists have spent decades trying to uncover the treasures and remains of this once great civilization.

Based on what is known, one of the greatest mysteries is why the Zapotec have not received the same attention and place in history as other well-known civilizations. As one of the largest Mesoamerican civilizations at the time, they helped to shape and form the world the Conquistadors encountered upon their arrival. Rivaling the size and complexity of their Mayan neighbors, the Zapotec were innovators and intellectuals who created a society that was markedly similar to the kingdoms and social structures.

One of the greatest mysteries about this sophisticated civilization is what happened to it. Roughly 2,500 years ago they were thriving. And then they were gone. After taming an area that was dry and difficult to navigate, they disappeared with almost no traces of what happened. These people who considered themselves to be children of the gods appeared to have returned to the clouds from whence they came, but not without leaving hints and pieces for archaeologists to find and interpret. Coupled with the writings of the Conquistadors, historians and archaeologists have been fleshing out every aspect of the Zapotec. From their early history where they tamed the Valley of Oaxaca to the society that met with the Conquistadors, there are many secrets of this once great civilization that have been uncovered.

The Zapotec were a fascinating people. They give a fresh look and understanding to civilizations that were just as complex, structured, and regal as any of their Mesoamerican, South American, or European counterparts.

# Chapter 1 – Looking Back over Hundreds of Years

While the Zapotec civilization disappeared long ago, there are many remnants that show how influential and intelligent its people were at the height of its power. What is known about them today is based on a combination of the records left by the Conquistadors and educated guesses based on the remains of the civilization. Archeologists also have access to some descendants of the Zapotecs who still live in the Mesoamerica area. Although their knowledge of their past is limited, they have kept some myths and beliefs alive. There are still many unanswered questions, particularly about what led to the nearly complete disappearance of the entire civilization, but every day archeologists learn a little bit more about this fascinating civilization. .

While it is true that a wide gap will always remain in the understanding and truth about this ancient civilization, historians and archaeologists have worked with the knowledge that they have gained from the records left by the Conquistadors, the ruins and the descendants of the Zapotecs to build a comprehensive picture of the history, evolving social structures, politics, and daily lives of these people. Slowly, they have been constructing a timeline that extends over more than a millennium to capture the rise and decline of the Zapotec.

# The Cloud People

To understand the Zapotec civilization, it is essential to have some basic knowledge of their religious beliefs (a fact that is true of every civilization, no matter how modern or ancient). Their civilization began to form roughly 2,500 years ago. Ancient Egypt had already seen the peak of its power and Rome was a republic, but not yet an Empire. The evolution of the Zapotec civilization was similar to the rise and evolution of the Roman Empire. The primary difference between the two was that the Zapotecs did not seek to take over the known world; they primarily sought to build and expand their culture over the surrounding area. Once they expanded their empire until it began to touch another empire, they frequently worked to build a relationship with that culture instead of trying to dominate it.

The Romans and the Zapotecs employed politics as a way of expanding their empires, and then resorted to war when they encountered resistance to their expansion. The Romans dealt with smaller bands of resistance compared to the world of Mesoamerica. Without any real power to counter their military in Europe, the Romans spread across Europe and northern Africa. In contrast, the Zapotecs were not the only significant power in the region. Shortly before the arrival of the Conquistadors, the Zapotecs had resolved yet another conflict with the Aztec civilization that lived to the north.

Like the Romans, the Zapotecs believed their existence was closely tied to their Pantheon. They also thought the upper echelons of their society derived from the gods. No living human, not even the high priest, was able to talk directly to the creator of the world, but that did not mean that the Zapotecs were ignored by the creator. Instead of having direct contact with humans, the creator and other gods showed their concern for the Zapotecs by the gift of almost everything that people encountered. All things that moved were considered to be significant, from the animals that they ate to the plants they harvested to the clouds in the sky where their ancestors lived. They believed everything that moved had a spirit that was given to it by the creator. From their place in the clouds, the ancestors of the upper class would offer the prayers of the people, both upper class and commoners, working to improve the lives of the entire civilization.

The Conquistadors spent several years studying the Zapotec civilization, learning about their culture and trying to correlate it to their own. Many aspects of Zapotec life were almost identical to European elements, but some were unfamiliar. This led to misleading information and representation about the Zapotecs that archaeologists have had to dispel over time. This has proven to be tricky since the civilization itself was gone by 1600 AD. However, there are still some descendants of the Zapotecs who have their own understanding of what the different rights and rituals meant, based on the myths and beliefs that have been passed down. This difference in interpretation in the Zapotecs' actions has given rise to a lot of skepticism among experts, and they have begun to construct their ideas and theories based on their findings in the ruins of the civilization.

One of the most notable discrepancies between what the Conquistadors noted and how archeologists interpret the religion is the number of gods worshipped. The Conquistadors based their information on questions and surveys with members of the Zapotec nobility. When they talked with the different leaders and kings of various areas, the Spanish found that each one tended to have their own pantheon beneath the main gods. Based on what the descendants of the Zapotecs say and the hieroglyphs, it is much more likely the "gods" that differed between the different cities and regions were not considered gods by the Zapotecs. It is probable that the reverence shown to these figures was similar to the reverence shown by the Catholic Church to saints at about the same time. The Zapotecs believed it was the ancestors of the nobles who could talk to the gods on behalf of the people, and so the ancestors were treated with respect after their death.

Part of the misunderstanding could have been that the Conquistadors considered their god to be above them, so when the Zapotecs indicated the clouds, the meaning was less clear. The Zapotecs had as much reverence for the clouds as any other moving part of the Earth, but it was easy for the Spanish to misunderstand it when it was juxtaposed with their own religion. While the Spanish believed humans came from the dirt, the Zapotecs thought they were from the clouds and that some of them would return to the clouds when they died.

# The Oaxaca Valley

Referred to as the Valley of Oaxaca, the region where the Zapotec civilization thrived and worshipped was as much a testament to their intellect and abilities as it was a critical component in forming who they were. While civilizations in Europe and North Africa developed around fertile areas where water was plentiful, the Zapotecs opted for safety, setting into a region that was easier to fortify and defend. The rise of the Zapotec civilization at Monte Albán was the beginning of a shift from another minor civilization into something far more substantial and innovative.

The roots of what would become a dominant civilization in the region came from the area where the people decided to settle. Their first major city was San José Mogote, but it proved to be less than ideal because the Zapotecs were always at war with their neighbors in that area. With much of the best land already occupied, in about 500 BC the Zapotecs decided to move to a location that was at a higher elevation at the top of one of the mountains, which enabled them to keep an eye for any approaching travelers or hostile neighbors. The new city was Monte Albán, and it was nestled in the Valley of Oaxaca.

There was a good reason why this region had not been populated before the Zapotecs arrived. One of the most prominent features of the Valley of Oaxaca is the mountains that surround it. Visiting the site of Monte Albán provides a sense of what it must have been like for the original settlers in the region. It is difficult not to feel isolated, and the remoteness made trade exceptionally difficult. For a people who had been in perpetual war though, isolation was welcome.

Source: https://study.com/academy/lesson/why-is-monte-alban-historically-important.html

Another major drawback to this region was how arid it was. Although the climate is temperate in the Valley of Oaxaca, there is only about 500 mm of rain a year – that is 20 inches a year. For a people who relied on agriculture for food, this was inadequate to sustain a large population. The minuscule amount of rain fell primarily between May and September. Today, scientists consider the area to be in "permanent drought.". Despite the lack of rain, agriculture has always been an essential part of the region, as much today as it was when the Zapotecs thrived in the area. The Zapotecs used the latest in technology and innovation to ensure crops could thrive. The need to be innovative to survive was probably one of the reasons the Zapotecs were more advanced than many of the other civilizations in the region. Archeologists have uncovered almost 3,000 sites that prove just how successful the Zapotecs were at ensuring their agrarian livelihood.

# The Domain of the Cloud People

Like all civilizations, the boundaries and borders of the Zapotec civilization shifted and changed over time. In the beginning, the Zapotecs were divided into three groups based on where they resided. The Valley Zapotecs lived in the Valley of Oaxaca, which became the heart of the civilization. The second group is the Sierra Zapotecs, and they resided to the north of the valley. The third group was the Southern Zapotecs. Despite the name historians and archaeologists have given them, the Southern Zapotecs lived to the south and the east of the valley, and their area was around the Isthmus of Tehuantepec.

Many cities and towns were important to the culture. There were three capitals over the course of the Zapotec history: San José Mogote, Monte Albán, and Mitla. However, the cities of Dainzu, Lambityeco, Yagul, El Palmillo, and Zaachila played vital roles in the development and expansion of the Zapotec Empire.

After the Zapotecs had established the thriving city of Monte Albán, they began to conquer many of their neighbors by overpowering them with superior military power. Then, because they had a larger population, the Zapotecs were easily able to absorb the smaller, conquered villages into their culture. Often, they would focus on peaceful means of bringing villages and peoples into their civilization, such as arranged marriages and offering the use of their more advanced technologies to the less advanced neighbors around them. Whether out of fear or an interest in joining a larger defender, the smaller civilizations around Monte Albán were easily incorporated into the Zapotec Culture.

Over time, their influence stretched far beyond Monte Albán. It is difficult to know precisely how vast the empire was because the Zapotecs did not keep borders the same way that Europeans did. Civilizations blended, with people from different cultures living together on the boundaries. It was difficult to remain a small, independent state or city with so many competing civilizations trying to expand. However, the large civilizations worked together as much as they fought against one another. The relationship between the Zapotecs and Teotihuacans, a nearby civilization, was mostly positive. One of the exceptions was the Aztec civilization, a neighbor to the north of the Zapotecs that was more dominating than the other cultures in the area.

The Zapotecs also expanded through politics and marriage, similar to the traditions of European royalty, rather than always relying on military might. Despite this proclivity to more political conquest, they had a much larger and more advanced military structure than many of their neighbors. Having found their footing in Monte Albán, it was much easier for them to begin to pick up their smaller, less warlike neighbors. They were also talented political tacticians. During their war with the Aztecs, the Zapotecs made an agreement with the Mixtecs. The Mixtecs resided in an area of tropical lowlands near the Aztecs, and they were to attack the Aztecs while the Aztecs were passing through the Tehuantepec lowlands. In return, the Zapotecs would give the Mixtecs land. Since the area to be given was not specified before the assistance, the Zapotecs gave the Tehuantepec land unsuitable for habitation. Having lost the bloody seven months' struggle against the Aztecs, the Zapotecs negotiated a deal that did not remove too much of their influence from the region. One of the rulers of the Aztecs wed the ruler of the Zapotecs. The Aztecs were also given garrisons in the Valley of Oaxaca and would receive an annual tribute from the Zapotecs. The loss to the Aztecs was undoubtedly a blow to the Zapotecs, but it was not the catastrophe it could have been, especially when one considers how harshly the Aztecs had treated smaller cultures upon their defeat. Unlike the Zapotecs, the Aztec Empire began their wars with mercenaries and those who were accustomed to fighting. The Aztecs did not shy away from fighting, and they did not seek a new place to avoid fighting. When the Aztecs won a battle, their prisoners were almost always sacrificed, unlike the less wholesale practices of the Zapotecs. While the Zapotecs did sacrifice some of their prisoners, many became concubines or slaves, and one day they might be allowed to gain their freedom. The Zapotecs were good at turning losses, truces, and agreements in their favor through the use of skillful negotiation. Using Machiavellian tactics, they could build their empire and sustain it even in defeat.

Their ability to work situations to their advantage did not work against the Conquistadors, however. Nor could they counter the deadly diseases the Conquistadors brought that wiped out many of the natives in Mesoamerica.

# Chapter 2 – Understanding the Zapotecs in Phases

Each empire and vast civilization reaches its peak in phases, and the Zapotecs are no different. The relics and ruins have provided a wealth of information about the growth of the Zapotec people, enough data to allow much of the extensive history of the Zapotecs to be divided into different eras or phases.

The identified phases of the Zapotecs revolves around their capital city. Even though the Zapotecs were a civilization before moving to Monte Albán, they did not have the prestige or security that helped them to thrive after the move.

## The Founding of the Monte Albán

Archaeologists have found numerous implements and tools that suggest three civilizations were living in the Valley of Oaxaca, including the Zapotecs. The remains of weapons and other implements indicate the civilizations were at war with each other and the constant warring was probably the reason why the Zapotecs decided to relocate.

It was almost certainly a sense of danger that drove them from their homes. The number of security features that still surrounds their capital is an indication that protecting their people was a primary concern for the Zapotec civilization.

The Zapotecs' reach would eventually extend beyond Monte Albán, but the Zapotec people really began to thrive after its founding. Their superior fortifications gave them the security necessary to grow in other ways. Because of their extensive security around the exterior of the Monte Albán, they became one of the most advanced and innovative peoples in Mesoamerica and perhaps around the world. They would develop their own type of writing that is comparable to Egyptian Hieroglyphics (the Zapotec writing are also called hieroglyphics). None of this would have been possible had they remained in the wetter, more populous regions where they had lived before moving to Monte Albán.

## Monte Albán Phase 1

The first phase lasted for roughly 300 years, from 400 BC to 100 BC. During the early history of the city that would eventually become the capital of an entire civilization, life was a struggle. The rainfall was negligible, so they needed to ensure famine would not be a greater enemy than the two civilizations they had encountered before their move to the area. The former center of the civilization, San José Mogote, had proven to be difficult to defend and too close to neighbors with militaries as capable as the military of the Zapotecs. Monte Albán gave the Zapotecs a place where they could grow and develop with fewer outside threats. It also gave them time to build their military.

During this time, many other people outside of Monte Albán were tied to the Zapotec civilization. While they were not yet looking to expand their reach to the extent that they would in later phases, the Zapotecs did begin to pull people from the surrounding areas into their civilization. They were still in the early stages of their civilization, so their hierarchical structure was more fluid than it would be at the peak of the Zapotecs' power. The nation was beginning to be centralized around this one city that was secure from outside threats, but it was still in the early days and people were still determining their place in the culture and society. This was a time of growth and development, and many of the ideas and innovations that would help them thrive later began during this phase.

Many of the structures that can be seen today were built during this early stage. Once they were secure, the Zapotec began developing language, jewelry, and structures that were far more advanced than any they had previously produced. There are also many pots and ceramics from this time, showing how interested the people were in creating and defining themselves through art. One of the most interesting items from this period is called the whistling jar. By dividing a jar into two different sections, the Zapotecs were able to pour water and store it at the same time. As air pushed the water out of one chamber, the jar would whistle. The whistling jar would continue to be made over the course of the civilization's history. They also began to sculpt with jade and other precious materials. The delicate jewelry and pottery, as well as the easily identifiable style that marks their civilization, are still one of the most intricate and unique of its kind today. For those who would like to see examples of the buildings and artifacts, pictures are available on the internet or you can check for a museum near you to see them in person, if you can't visit the sites themselves.

# Monte Albán Phase 2

Phase 2 was a shorter period of time, lasting from about 100 BC to 100 AD, but it was a time of rapid growth and development of Monte Albán. With the borders of their capital secure, religion, art, and innovation rapidly expanded. It also marked a time when the Zapotecs began to incorporate a broader range of areas from the towns and villages near Monte Albán. Much of the expansion was achieved through military might, and not through political savvy. Compared to their previous locations, it was much easier to take control of their neighbors because the towns and villages around Monte Albán were smaller and less militarily stable. With higher numbers and better strategies, the Zapotecs could grow their civilization through the use of military might similar to that of the early days of the Roman Empire.

Also, like the Romans, the Zapotecs allowed those they conquered to retain some level of autonomy. Annexing these territories was meant to be a way of extending their reach, supplies, and power, so the Zapotecs took a more laissez-faire approach to managing their conquered territories. By submitting to the Zapotecs, the annexed areas could retain some of their own laws and power structures. Many of the conquered people lived in areas outside of the valley, but not so far from Monte Albán that they would have been difficult to monitor and trade with.

The signs of the expansion during this time are primarily in the relics discovered in the areas around Monte Albán during this 200-year period. Pottery, jewelry, and other everyday items found in these areas that were conquered indicated roughly when they became part of the larger civilization because the items were significantly different to the works that came from earlier periods It also appeared the changes in style and design were sudden, suggesting the people were being incorporated quickly into the Zapotec civilization. The elegance and intricacies of the Zapotec artisans were well worth imitating as well. As the styles of these items was similar but not identical, archeologists have postured that these items show as much a history of the Zapotecs' expansion as they do about the everyday lives of the people of these smaller territories.

# Monte Albán Phase 3

This period lasted from 200 AD to 900 AD, and it proved to be a time of military might and the centralization of power around the capital. Monte Albán was the center of the Zapotec empire, but it was not the capital of their religion. There was not a real separation of their religion and power structures, but these two power structures were each large enough to require their own capitals.

The military strength the Zapotecs had flexed during Monte Albán phase 2 was proven to be highly effective during the third era. Over the 700 years of phase 3, Monte Albán became the largest human settlement in the region. It is estimated the city may have been the home to over 25,000 people during this phase. The Zapotecs also included more than 1,000 settlements as part of their empire, with Monte Albán as its center. This was the time when the rulers were focused on expanding well beyond the valley, conquering areas as far north as Quiotepec and as far south as Chiltepec. Just as other empires found themselves extended too far with inadequate resources to sustain their power structure, the Zapotecs found themselves up against other civilizations with greater military capabilities than their own. The most notable adversary was the Aztec.

However, no central city can sustain the kinds of growth and innovation that Monte Albán experienced during phase 3. By the end of this phase, the city was in decline as the people became complacent and their ideas began to stagnate. While Monte Albán would still be a significant city for the Zapotecs, it ceased to be the capital around 900 AD. Mitla would become the empire's center, although it would never be quite as large or as influential as Monte Albán was at its peak.

## Monte Albán Phase 4

Monte Albán still played a significant role in the empire from 900 AD to 1350 AD. However, people from other civilizations began to make it their place of residence. With more people of varied beliefs and backgrounds in a city that relied on people acting in a similar way, the city started to lose itself. Its influence was significantly reduced as Mitla attracted many of the people in the upper echelons of the Zapotec society.

With the loss of some of their influential figures and the introduction of people from other cities and regions, Monte Albán began to lose some of its culture and control. The people who controlled the city were no longer people who necessarily grew up there. This meant that power began to be shared with people who held different beliefs and social focus than the native Zapotec population. The more the power within the city was distributed among other groups, the less power the city had within the empire. Though Monte Albán continued to be important, it was no longer the center of the civilization and its role was less critical.

By this time, the civilization had extended itself too far and had reached a tipping point. Unable to maintain its once dominant capital, the Zapotecs began to lose control over regions on their borders. The losses were not significant at this point, but it was a sign that the once great empire was no longer able to sustain itself as it once had. The people had become too complacent and self-important, a sign that the empire was crumbling. The empire forgot what made it great and internal power struggles became prevalent and its decline was assured. When Rome fell, the Roman Empire ended, and the Byzantine Empire began. Even today, it is easy to see the decline of nations because of how rapidly things deteriorate in their capitals. The fall of Monte Albán signaled the beginning of the end of the Zapotec empire.

## Monte Albán Phase 5

The last phase of Monte Albán lasted for less than 200 years from 1350 AD to 1521 AD. By this point, the city no longer enjoyed the power and innovation that had been at its core through much of its existence.

It was also a difficult time for the Zapotec people as they went to war with their more powerful neighbors, the Aztecs. By the time the Aztecs emerged victorious over the Zapotecs, Monte Albán was no longer the mighty city it had once been. Given the location of the city, it is possible that some of the decline could have come from drought and other natural problems that would have devastated the inhabitants of Monte Albán. With power no longer centralized among a few leaders who understood the importance of the structures and irrigation, the people would have been forced to leave, although probably not all at once. The power structure would have been far less resilient than the early structure that had seen the growth of the city. With so many surrounding areas needing attention and protection, it would have been too much to manage internal and external problems. This was the city that the Conquistadors would have discovered, although even then it was still a majestic place.

## The Promise of Tomorrow

The Zapotecs had accepted their defeat at the hands of the Aztecs by 1515, but they were still mostly independent. Having successfully negotiated the terms of peace, the Zapotecs were not defeated in quite the same way as those they had conquered earlier.

Then the Conquistadors arrived, and everything changed again. For a few years, while the Aztecs were fighting the invaders, there was hope that the Zapotecs could return to their previous lives from before their loss to the Aztecs. For a short period, they could hope for a return to the power and control they once held. Then the Conquistadors turned their attention to the Zapotecs.

# Chapter 3 – Early Agrarian Roots and the Building of a Civilization

The beginnings of one of the most influential civilizations in Mesoamerica were humble. In the early days, there was little to mark the Zapotecs as being any different to their neighbors. They transitioned from being nomads to farmers, then from farmers into small villages. Once they began to live in larger and larger groups though, the shape of the Zapotec society began to differ from those civilizations around them. While they fought, the Zapotecs were also interested in progressing beyond the day to day lives. They sought to record information through writing and design tools to make life easier. Their jewelry, pottery, and other works of art were more distinctive with the addition of writing and images of their gods. At some point, their desire to create clashed with the reality of their lives. The daily routine in a small village or on farms might have been enough if the area had been more peaceful. It was this discontentment with their constant fighting that eventually led to the empire.

It may be that the Zapotecs learned from their early struggles how best to handle more warlike neighbors. Given how they seemed to seek a peaceful resolution later on, despite how powerful they were at their peak, the early days likely formed much of the way they thought about war. The constant state of fighting would have made it difficult to fully implement any tactics because battle was as much a part of their routines as farming. It was only after they moved, that it became clear just how capable the Zapotecs were. Their new capital was one of the most heavily fortified cities in the region.

## From Nomad to Villagers

Five thousand years ago, when the Ancient Egyptians were just starting to form their kingdom, the future inhabitants of the Valley of Oaxaca were still roaming across the lands, but they were beginning to take a different outlook on survival. Archeologists cannot say for sure when the nomads finally decided to settle down in one location, but early agriculture gave the people of the region a new way to live. Before 1700 BC, the ancestors to the Zapotecs had become farmers, though they tended only to grow what was needed to survive on their own. Providing enough food to feed an entire community was still not something that most groups of humans practiced. A farmer grew only enough food to feed his family, and others were left to fend for themselves if they could not grow as much food as they needed for themselves.

Then between 1700 BC and 1200 BC, the farmers began to band together to provide support and assistance to an increasingly larger population. Living together provided safety from predators and other humans.

Because of the shift in thinking, the point of agriculture began to shift too. While it is not certain why the early Zapotecs decided to start focusing their agriculture on growing maize (also known as corn), there is adequate evidence the shift occurred after they began to live together in larger groups. This suggests that one of the reasons for the change in farming was a desire to feed more people with less effort. It also provided the farmers with products that they could trade for other goods.

One thing that is known about the shift is that the larger groups recognized that land was difficult to clear, particularly as larger groups of humans joined together. That meant the clearing process needed to be worthwhile. At some point, the early Zapotecs had begun to determine what food would make the most sense for a growing population. Maize was their answer.

As they needed to tend an increasingly larger area of farmed land, people began to take on more specialized jobs. There were still hunters for game, but there were also those who planted, weeded, and harvested the crops. Others stayed with the children and elderly. They would make tools and care for those who where in need.

Over time, the groups became larger, so more people lived in close proximity and worked together to accomplish more in less time. There are remains of the early tools, including pottery, that show that the early Zapotecs had shifted from their early days to the more complex village structure. Their homes were far more basic, with few to no remains of the structures, but the high concentration of artifacts and burials prove the shift to a unified approach to survival had been successful by 3,000 years ago.

# The Early Structuring of Society

The ancestors of the Zapotecs did not have lives that were distinctly different from any of the other cultures growing up around them. Their lives evolved from nomadic to farmers to villagers. In the early days, men began to fight each other to run their villages. Called the Big Man, the chief of a village was responsible for raiding other villages, forming alliances with other villages, and inspiring his people against enemies. Once he died, alliances and enemies disappeared because they were based on the Big Man and the people he competed with.

This began to change around 1200 BC when leadership began to solidify around more than just the strongest person in a village. During this time heredity began to play a role in a person's role, and classes of people began to form within villages. It meant a shift in their religion and the way they viewed the world.

To the early Zapotecs, two critical entities were fundamental to their beliefs: Sky and Earth. These were considered to be supernatural entities. Earth was mostly benevolent, but it did not like being treated poorly, including burning and digging on its surface. When it was angered, it would let the Zapotecs know that it was angry by shaking. The result of Earth's rage was an earthquake.

The Sky was removed from the problems of humans and was the home of celestial spirits, particularly their Zapotec ancestors. Being removed from humans did not mean that Sky was not displeased by them though. When Sky was angry about human actions, it would show that anger through lightning.

These entities began to be added to pottery around 1150 BC, indicating that the deities played a more critical role in the life of the people. Around this time, humans began to be shown as descendants of Earth and Sky, and like European royalty, people started to believe the leaders had their positions because of their ancestry. With this subtle shift in thinking, hierarchies began to form. Males began to be depicted as descendants on pottery and other relics from the time and those believed to be related to Earth and Sky were buried with the works that showed their status. The lineage always progressed through males. Women were not depicted as being descendants of the supernatural entities at this point.

# A Move to Hierarchies and away from Autonomy

With some people claiming divine ancestry, there was more justification for someone to take control over every aspect of village life. Someone who was not recognized as being divine was not allowed to be in charge. While the Big Man could demand obedience from his people, his words did not hold any sway over other villages. When a leader began to claim divine lineage, it gave his people the right to demand the loyalty and obedience of other villages. If the surrounding villages resisted, violence would ensue. If the village of the divine leader succeeded, it was seen as a sign his words were considered the divine will. Villages were more inclined to accept the new social order and demands of a conquering people when their leader was thought to be related to the gods. The victory was seen as being the will of a greater being, so the conquered people accepted their fate more willingly.

The children of a successful leader claiming divine lineage would automatically be treated with reverence, making it more difficult to deny each successive leader. As the divine leader took wives from new villages, the divine lineage would spread to the other villages, giving them a vested interest in the hierarchy. Over time, people ceased to question the divine claims and accepted this as the proper order of the world.

Signs of the loss of village autonomy were found in the ruins of the city of San José Mogote. The first capital of the Zapotec Empire reflected the hierarchy in a way that the satellite villages did not. The remains of many buildings that were not present in the other villages indicate that San José Mogote was considered to be more important, meaning more effort was placed on creating structures that would last longer. Better materials were used to construct the buildings, and the beginnings of more ornate designs showed the reverence that was given to those who resided in those structures. Many of these materials did not originally come from San José Mogote; rather, they were brought in from the satellite villages. The fact that San José Mogote had such structures and the villages did not suggests the leaders could demand the materials. The satellite villages acquiesced, providing whatever was requested instead of using it for their own structures and products. With San José Mogote being the home of the leaders and the place to which homage was paid, the villages in the surrounding areas were no longer allowed to make their own decisions.

The leader of the Zapotecs lived in San José Mogote, a place that was better fortified and stocked than any of the other villages within the region. Within San José Mogote, there were members of the nobility who were related to the leader or who were related to other, lesser leaders with divine lineage. All members of the nobility were believed to be descended from Earth or Sky, and they were treated accordingly. Some of those of divine descent lived in the surrounding villages. The villages that they lived in were usually larger than most of the other villages, but not as grand as San José Mogote. They were the leaders of these villages, and they took their orders from the central leader. Smaller villages had minor leaders who would follow the orders of the leader of the larger villages. This provided a chain of command that removed the autonomy of all villages that were part of the growing Zapotec civilization.

## The Rise of Alliances and Competition

The Zapotecs were not the only civilization taking shape at this time. They had consolidated control of their region under a divine ruler, but other leaders were making the same types of claims and building their hierarchies. Unlike the Big Man who could shame any rivals into following him, leaders were now faced with having to prove they had a superior lineage. To resolve these kinds of disputes, the leader had two possible courses of action: form alliances or compete with their adversary.

The Zapotecs began facing these kinds of challenges around 850 BC to 700 BC And the challenges were not always from external sources.

The people within the villages were part of the hierarchy with their ancestry being easier to track than the ancestry of rulers claiming divine blood without evidence. It was much easier to track lineage from leaders through their offspring, and this resulted in some members of the nobility jockeying for better status when they were of less prestigious descent. The internal hierarchy further solidified during this time.

More interesting than the challenges within the San José Mogote hierarchy were the relationships the growing civilization had with the surrounding neighbors who were too large to force into submission.

Although fighting was indeed an option, it appears the Zapotecs were more inclined to form alliances, a tactic they continued to use throughout most of the duration of the empire. It is supposed that alliances were formed through hypogamy. Hypogamy is the practice of sending a woman of higher rank to a subordinate community leader where they are then wed to solidify the alliance. Given that she was of higher status than the leader she married, this automatically elevated the status of the leader within the hierarchy. It also meant he was indebted to the family who gave him the bride, creating a much closer connection between the subordinate village and the primary noble family in San José Mogote. This same method of forming alliances was common in Europe up until recent centuries. In Europe, it got to the point where royalty was mostly inbred, sometimes with disastrous consequences. For the Zapotecs during this time, that was not as much of a problem because there were far fewer blood relations between the villages and San José Mogote.

Large feasts were another way of building alliances, a method the Zapotecs almost certainly used. However, there is little to indicate how these feasts worked to do more than impress the villages. It could have been a way of showing off how well their harvest had done and their robust stocks of meat. Their primary source of domesticated food appears to have been dog, showing that canines were not held in the same kind of regard in Mesoamerica as they were in Europe where they were more often used as companions.

# War and the Beginnings of Writing

While a bit ironic, it is perhaps not unsurprising that the evidence of both war and writing began at around the same time. With pottery being a primary means of seeing how the society changed over time, around this time, words and depictions of wars began to appear on the artifacts that were found at the archeological sites.

When the Zapotec chief fought with the other civilizations, it was usually over resources and goods. At this time, none of the budding civilizations had adequate military or resources to occupy another area, so their primary goal was not conquest. When they could not continue to protect a village or area, chiefs would pull back their military, abandoning the villages to their fate.

It is notable that during this time, none of the growing chiefdoms had any interest in the region where the Zapotec civilization would eventually take root and thrive. As many cultures were unwilling to learn to work the arid region and the mountains and the valleys were considered to be too remote, this area was largely ignored in the struggle to gain more resources.

While the writing at this time was rudimentary, it was still a departure from merely adding images to the pottery and structures. There was more repetition of intricate works similar to the hieroglyphs associated with Ancient Egypt. Of course, the Zapotec hieroglyphs were unique to their civilizations, but it is clear that they were beginning to record thoughts and words in a pattern that aligns with writing. There was less writing found on the structures that have been found in San José Mogote, but the new capital bears many examples of structures with writing following the migration.

# Chapter 4 – Religion, Myths, and Power

The Zapotec religion was complex and varied, and they held their ancestors in reverence in a way that is commonly associated with Native Americans. With the development of the civilization through leaders who claimed divine heritage, there was no separation of church and state. The social structure that a person was born into was the one they would be in until the day they died. Politics were equally complicated, although the Zapotecs believed that their rulers were descended from supernatural beings.

## The Zapotec Pantheon

There were two primary supernatural beings the Zapotecs believed in: Sky and Earth. These two beings were mostly benevolent, but when they were angry, they would let the Zapotecs know about their anger through earthquakes and lightning. These beings were given names and were depicted on many of their artworks and stories. The rain god, Cocijo, ensured they had adequate precipitation in the less arid areas, although he was not crucial in the capital, Monte Albán, because it was dry and received only about two inches of rainfall a year. However, they did rely on the deity to keep their water sources full. Coquihani was their god of light.

Lesser gods were responsible for the more common aspects of life, such as fertility and agriculture. These gods were both male and female. In looking over their writings, you can tell a deity's gender because it is reflected in the clothing worn: men wear capes and women wear skirts. Very little is known about them, apart from the fact that there were minor gods.

The pantheon is not nearly as extensive as the Conquistadors initially believed. Where they had interpreted many of the prayers and sacrifices to deities, it appears that many of these were actually to ancestors, and not deities. No human could talk directly to Cocijo or Coquihani, so they had to ask their ancestors to intercede on their behalf. It appears that mainly only the members of the nobility had ancestors who could interact with the gods because commoners returned to the Earth when they died, and not to the sky. However, it is possible that commoners prayed to their own families as well, particularly if they needed to communicate with Cocijo.

## Rituals, Sacrifices, and Myths

While they did acknowledge the Zapotec king, the priests had their own internal structure with class being less relevant for interactions. Since the Zapotecs were firm believers in their religion, the priests and other religious figures were held in high regard and wielded their own power. While they never tried to rival the king, they were obeyed by the people. As the king consolidated his power, so too did the priests, and they spread their decisions to the priests of the other villages and settlements.

The deities required regular sacrifices, and these were given based on the time of year and current events. For example, the first warrior caught in battle was sacrificed to the gods as a way of thanking them. Others captured in the fight would become slaves or sacrifices depending on their usefulness. Officers of the opposition military were usually eaten. It is not entirely clear why officers were eaten; however, it is probable that the Zapotecs believed that other civilizations derived from different gods. Since everything that moved had a spirit and the Zapotecs believed that officers were descended from the gods, eating the officers might have been a way of getting closer to their gods. Sacrifices, including humans, were made on religious holidays.

Small animals and harvests were also offered up to the gods and made up a larger percentage of the sacrifices. However, the priests made the most frequent sacrifices, cutting themselves and adding their blood to the ceremonies. Special tools were made for the priests to cut their own tongues and pierce their ears. While it is not known exactly why their own blood was considered essential, priests would often cut or pierce themselves during ceremonies, giving up a little bit of themselves. It was likely one of the reasons why they were held in high regard. Since the priests had dedicated their lives to the gods they worshipped, it is likely they gave their own blood as a way of returning some of their spirits back to their gods. Little is known about the reasons for the bloody tradition, and it is particularly interesting because many of the ceremonies seemed to demand so much from the priests. While there were other kinds of sacrifices, it appears that priests frequently gave more of themselves than they took from others. The number of obsidian knives and stingray spines in the remains of temples shows just how important it was for the priests to give of themselves since these tools were not used on the sacrifices.

The Zapotecs had their own myths about how the world began. It is perhaps surprising that they believed in a superior being who created the world, but whom no one could talk to. This being did not appear to play a role in their worship because no human was able to interact; not even their ancestors who resided in the clouds. According to the Zapotecs, the creator had allowed for humans to be born of the rocks in the Valley of Oaxaca. This not only gave them a history, but it proved the region rightfully belonged to the Zapotecs. There were other versions of the creation myth though. Some taught that humans descended from the animals who lived in the region. Ocelots and jaguars were considered to be the most common sources for humans.

However, the most common myth was that the leaders of the Zapotecs were direct descendants of supernatural beings. Once they died, the leaders would return to the clouds, where they would communicate with the gods. Commoners would continue to show reverence to their ancestors, but the ancestors of the noble class were revered by all. This myth is the source of the people's name, "Cloud People."

# Distribution of Power

In the larger areas, such as Monte Albán, power was centered around the nobility, particularly the ruler of the civilization. The Conquistadors noted that the social structure and power were tied together, and they even compared it to the social and power structures that were common in Europe at the time. Some positions were comparable to those of counts, dukes, earls, princes, and other strata of the power hierarchy.

However, the further from these populous regions archeologists go, the more evidence they find of levels of autonomy. During the Monte Albán Phases 1 and 2, there was a high level of autonomy and independent states within the civilization. It was only during the Monte Albán Phase 3 that a more rigid system was put in place, and power was removed from these areas. With Monte Albán as its seat of power, the Zapotecs at their peak had one of the largest domains in Mesoamerica.

During Monte Albán Phase 3, the Zapotec king was the sole seat of power, and his word was law. The king made all critical decisions, and his word was spread to the villages.

Monte Albán was the center of political power over the majority of the civilization. While the political will and power came from the capital, the city of Mitla was the seat of the religious authority.

Toward the end of the civilization, the political power also shifted toward Mitla, but it had long been accustomed to a different kind of power by that time. Part of the remains of this one formidable population center was a palace. Made mostly of mud and stone, the palace still has elegant carvings and decorations that indicate it was an important structure.

There are many remnants of the buildings where the powerful lived, including the palace in Mitla. However, the temples where the people worshipped are rarely found in good condition. Archaeologists often have to search hard the find the ruins of these structures because during battles and wars the Zapotecs and their neighbors would always burn the temples of their opponents. This was meant to anger the gods against the people for failing to protect their temples. With many of the civilizations long gone, their temples rarely remain as those would have been the first things destroyed by the people who came after them. The temples were as extravagant as the palaces. Like many other civilizations in the area, the Zapotecs favored pyramids for their temples, and the tops were adorned with the deities that the temples were dedicated to worshiping.

Some ruins offer information about other aspects of life. From sports and competitions to government buildings, archeologists can get an idea of how power was distributed over the civilization. There are signs that the further from Monte Albán they explore, the more unique the pottery and buildings are. Toward the borders, the buildings and facades were blended with the neighboring civilizations, showing there were times of alliances and a symbiotic relationship between the Zapotecs and many of their neighbors. People today think of the natives of the continents as being warlike and barbaric, but the reality is that they were not so different from the Europeans. The Zapotecs, in particular, tended to prefer alliances and politics over fighting and war, probably because they remembered their early days of constant fighting. They were also skillful negotiators, so relying on politics to resolve conflicts would have been far easier for them.

## Determining the Next Leader

While it was not possible for a commoner to gain a position of power, the children of the leader could vie for the position following the death of the leader. Archeologists can identify the position of the princes from the objects buried with them. Many of the items included writings that signified the son's place within the noble family. The position of the sons was indicated on their tombs, with the extended fingers of the depicted prince indicating his status and birth order. The first-born son was depicted as having an extended thumb, showing that he was the likely heir to the nation. If the depiction showed the prince's index finger extended, it indicated he was the second son of the king. Each consecutive extended finger showed the birth order of the child depicted.

The first-born son to the king's first wife usually became the next leader, but it was not always guaranteed. To become king, the sons would have to prove they were capable leaders. They had to meet five obligations.

1.  The future king would need to take captives who would be sacrificed when he was elevated to the kingship. This proved that he was capable of taking control and he was strong enough to lead.

2.  His blood had to be sacrificed to the gods, showing he was willing to give himself to the people and their gods at his own personal cost.

3.  The heir had to sponsor the building of a new facility. These buildings were usually some of the most varied, and some of the most remarkable structures stem from this requirement. The type of building and its intricacies provided a look into what the princes considered significant.

4. The heir also needed to commission a monument that would be dedicated to one of his ancestors. Like the facility, this monument provided a unique look into the minds of the princes.

5. He also had to seek the support and approval from others in power. Rulers in neighboring areas had to agree to his ascension. This helped to reduce the risk of wars and problems as it established a level of trust between the Zapotec ruler and others.

One of the most notable buildings that remains in Monte Albán was a result of a prince proving his worth. Each potential king contributed to the society in a way that was unique. Some focused on the buildings while others concentrated on relationships. Whichever approach they took, the future king could not simply relax knowing his place was secure. By ensuring that the prince would take care of his people, the Zapotecs looked to ensure their civilization would continue to grow and thrive instead of becoming complacent. This is perhaps one of the reasons why they could continue with their innovations for so long.

# The Dead

The Zapotecs treated their dead with as much respect as any other advanced civilization. There were entire structures dedicated to the deceased, and they were buried with gifts and treasures to ensure they had their things in the afterlife. Many of the items with which they were buried left hints about who they were, as well as the way they were buried.

Entire areas of cities and villages were dedicated to taking care of the deceased. Rituals were long and complicated, particularly for the leaders and people with power. The complexes within cities were large, allowing for the increased number of dead who had to be tended to on a regular basis. Elegant and elaborate tombs were covered in delicate motifs that told the stories of the people who were buried. The stories were varied, including telling of a brave warrior who met his end in battle, priests who carried out the will of the gods, and rulers who contributed to the civilization in their own ways. Tombs were built underground, providing a more stable resting place in the mountains.

# Chapter 5 – A Familiar, Tiered Society

Once the Zapotecs had settled on the top of Monte Albán, they already had a relatively rigid hierarchy that determined a person's potential positions in life. There were two distinct classes, and it was impossible to cross from one to the other, with one exception – there was less class distinction among the members of their religious hierarchy. And the priests wielded their own kind of power, just as they did in Europe.

## The Royal Family and Class

As the Conquistadors noted during the years when they observed and questioned the Zapotecs, the social structure for the ruling class was similar to that of the ruling classes that the Conquistadors were familiar with in Europe. A person was either born into the class, or they weren't – there was no way to transition between the two. They practiced strict class endogamy; they only married within their own class.

At the top of this class was the king and his primary wife. Other members of their family had titles to distinguish where they were in the ranking. The upper class did have different levels, with people in the highest strata being the ones most closely related to the ruler, but they could marry anyone else within the upper class. Some marriages were arranged to forge closer bonds between the ruling class, their neighbors, and other villages within the civilization.

The homes of the upper class were far nicer and located in places that offered a better view of the people. Families often continued to live together even after marriage. They had locations called royal houses for large families that were of a more distant relation to the king. The royal palace was for the king and his immediate family. These structures were built on a stone foundation and the walls made of adobe brick to provide the sturdiest buildings for the nobles.

The upper class commissioned many of the structures in the cities as a way of contributing to the society. When Monte Albán was first settled, the rulers had the entire top of the mountain flattened so the city could be built on it. This also gave them a strategic advantage over any invaders because they could see anyone advancing while they were still far away. Such innovation was part of the foundation of the requirements for the ruling class to push the civilization to strive beyond the norms that were established elsewhere. One of the largest areas in the city was atop where the mountain was leveled, and it was known as the Great Plaza. This area likely served as a place for entertainment and commerce. Other facilities and buildings surrounded it. There was also a stadium nearby, as well as several temples.

One of the remaining structures that is the most impressive is The Conquest Slab in Monte Albán. The facility is designed in the shape of an arrowhead, and the walls are scrawled with hieroglyphs that extend nearly all the way around the facility. Archaeologists believe the stories carved into the walls detailed the provinces the Zapotecs conquered, based on the figures carved into each of the 40 stones. The hieroglyphs on each of the stones include a carved head believed to be the ruler of that province because of the elaborate headdress they wore in the image.

The royal Zapotecs were the rulers of the people and held the offices. All official government employees were from this class, and it does not appear they held other types of positions within the society.

Apart from their homes, the noble class was allowed to wear better clothing than commoners. They had colorful mantles and loincloths that let people know their status which made it easier to show proper respect to those in the upper class. Their clothing was also made of cotton, which was more comfortable in the temperate region. In addition to more colorful cotton, members of the royal class could also wear feathers in their clothing and feather headdresses. Their jewelry was typically made of jade, as was their lip plug and ear ornaments. These accessories were not available for use by commoners. When they were called to war, nobles were given a quilted cotton armor that offered better protection than the clothing the commoners usually wore. However, it also marked the nobles for their enemies to recognize when they had captured someone of the higher class. This could mean that the nobles would be traded or purchased, or it could also mean their enemies would eat them.

Nobles also had a different diet. They received some of the best of the crops, and their meats included large game, such as deer and elk. Commoners joined them for their hunts, working to scare the prey out of their hiding place while the nobles killed the animals. Nobles also have the privilege of eating chocolate, something else that was denied to commoners.

## The Commoner Class and Its Layers

The second class belonged to the commoners, and it included everyone who was not a part of the noble family. This class was far more varied than the noble class as it contained anyone who was not considered to be related to the gods. At the bottom of this class were the slaves who came from the conquered nations. At the top of the commoner class were the successful merchants who could have more wealth than some of the minor noble family members. However, they were not allowed to marry members of the upper class, even for financial gain because the Zapotecs did not believe the two classes were equal. When the member of one of the noble families died, they would become ancestors who could speak to the gods for the people. No matter how much wealth or prestige the merchants earned, they would return to the Earth once they died. This belief in the afterlife kept the Zapotecs from intermarrying outside of their class.

Slaves could earn their freedom and become productive members of the society. Some slaves would be given to the nobles to be concubines, and others became sacrifices to the Zapotec gods. Those who earned their freedom would be allowed to marry anyone within the commoner class because there was no real distinction made between the wealthiest merchants and slaves. Those who were used as concubines would provide descendants to the nobles, but it is unclear what the place of those offspring was within the society.

The homes for commoners were far simpler than the homes of nobles. Homes were small, although large families probably lived in them. The occupations of the common class were diverse. The merchants provided a bridge between the Zapotecs and other civilizations since they would travel farther than nearly any other member of the civilization to complete their work. Many of the commoners who lived in cities were artisans and entertainers. Some were weavers who made beautiful clothing for the nobles and less costly and elaborate garb for the successful merchants. Musicians, dancers, and sculptors stayed employed in building the culture, and it is their work that has survived for archaeologists to find today. There were peddlers who were different from merchants because they operated on a much smaller scale. Some peddlers traveled long distances and brought much-needed goods to more remote areas, and others who worked solely within the cities or a small group of villages. Diviners and healers provided help for determining a person's future and for curing ailments.

There were also those who were innovators that worked for the betterment and advancement of the society. Engineers developed new ways to accomplish difficult or repetitive tasks, and they ensured the development and maintenance of the irrigation system, so there were no issues within the cities and large villages about water. From developing the first written language in Mesoamerica to creating the first irrigation system to improving the products such as pottery, jewelry and buildings that were used every day, the Zapotecs made good use of those who sought to further the culture.

The occupations of commoners were similar to those of other societies of the period, although they were not as oppressed as commoners were in some nations. They were free to act according to their own needs and whims as long as it did not harm the society. This level of freedom is one of the reasons why the Zapotecs could advance their civilization and technology so much further and faster than their neighbors. Many nations based their advancement on conquering and expanding their reach. The Zapotecs created a comfortable world for themselves and ensured that it could be sustained before they began their expansion. Because they had a strong commoner class, the Zapotecs could encourage people to do more and strive harder. By keeping the commoner class from being further divided into rigid subgroups, it gave people who had less wealth the hope that they could work towards getting more. With a marriage pool that was much larger than the limited choices of marriage partners from rigid class subsets possible in Europe, it allowed people to choose their own path and find more suitable partners for their lives.

Men of all social levels could marry more than one woman, but most commoners could not afford to have multiple wives. Mostly wealthy merchants were the only men who could afford to have more than one wife and numerous children. They had larger homes, but the homes were not nearly as elegant or sturdy as the homes of the nobles. Nor were they eligible for higher office.

The clothing of commoners was also significantly different to the clothing of the nobles. The commoners used agave fibers in plain colors for their mantles and loincloths. Their jewelry was also less noticeable and ornate and were not made from precious metals or gems.

## The Religious Order

Technically, the religious order was not a separate class, but the strict hierarchy prevalent in society was far less noticeable among the priests. The noble classes held higher stations within the religious chain of command, but the nobles were harder to distinguish from commoners within the temples because they were much more similarly adorned. All priests were expected to hold religious ceremonies and perform rituals, so that the roles of nobles and commoners within the Zapotec religious order were far less rigid than it was in society. Priests of noble blood were also expected to give more blood during ceremonies, as well as consume more hallucinogenic plants than the priests who were commoners. The roles of the upper-class priests were more important than a commoner priest's role, but they did perform many of the same tasks and duties. A commoner in society could never be confused for a noble person because they did not hold the same jobs or even similar jobs; but within the religion orders, lineage was less important than duty to the gods.

The king received religious training, giving him a better understanding of the religion he was to represent during his reign. Typically his religious training would last for a few years.

At the top of the religious hierarchy was the high priest, and the Conquistadors considered him to be comparable to the Pope. His role was largely fulfilled from the temple in Milta, and it was likened to the Vatican in Rome. The home of the high priest was beautifully crafted and well maintained over the years. With two pillars flanking the front door to the outer room of the temple, it was imposing and helped put people in the right frame of mind as they stepped into the temple.

While nobles were placed in higher positions within the religious order, many commoners were instrumental in performing some of the most important ceremonies. It is perhaps a result of the members of the religious orders being held in such high regard that a commoner who chose to join the priesthood was considered to be nearly as valuable of those born of noble blood. In the Zapotec religious structure, there was equality for men.

The rituals that commoners could perform included adding their blood to the ceremonies when it was required. Their blood was considered an acceptable part of the sacrifice. They also participated in mind-altering parts of the ceremonies, eating hallucinogenic mushrooms and jimson weed to induce the right state of mind for the ceremonies. Fasting was practiced for long periods of time to keep the spirit clear, and the commoners could sacrifice slaves, children, and dogs just like the priests who had higher lineage. Apart from the most notable ceremonies, there were very few distinctions between noble and commoner priests, something that even the Conquistadors found unexpected. The blurring of social structure within religion demonstrated that birth status was less instrumental than a willingness to serve.

# Chapter 6 – A Day in the Life of the Zapotecs

Trying to decipher what a day looked like for one of the Zapotec people is a unique challenge. The way the world looked changed based on the social structure that a person was born into and where they lived within the civilization. Just as the experiences of someone living in Mexico City today are significantly different from someone, who lives in Catalina or a small unknown village in modern-day Mexico, a typical day in the Zapotec civilization depended on a person's location and status.

## Wide Variety of Living Standards

The Zapotec cities were in the most populous regions of the civilization, and the days of the people who lived in the city were far more varied than those who lived outside of them. In the cities, there were people who had never worked a field of crops because they had more specialized jobs. Naturally, there were priests and other religious figures who spent their days in prayer and sacrifice. There were artisans and warriors who focused on their tasks. Still, they could live more comfortably than lower nobles who did not have the same resources. There were beggars and poor people within the cities too, and their experience was significantly different than many of the other citizens because they did not have the resources to contribute or improve their situation. Slaves were also common in cities, but depending on the tasks they were assigned, they could earn their freedom and become part of the society. Concubines typically did not leave their role, but a slave for a merchant or other commoner could often work to earn their freedom.

In the areas away from the cities, the primary occupation was farming. They lived in large and small villages of varying levels of wealth and comfort. They lived in mountain settlements acting as a stopping point for travelers and merchants while eking out a living in less than ideal circumstances. There were ranches and rural areas where farming occupied the vast majority of the day for the people who lived and worked there.

Hunters were still common across every area and in every region. The nobles would go out to hunt large game, taking commoners out with them to beat bushes to drive the wildlife into the open. Commoners could hunt anything that wasn't big game, such as jackrabbits, squirrels, and other small animals.

As you can see, the experience of each Zapotec was unique to their environment and status. It was easy to recognize someone of the higher status just by looking at them. The commoners may have had less brilliant clothing, but they were free to live as they pleased. The only restrictions were that they could not intermarry with the nobles, and they could not hold higher government positions. However, commoners could hold minor government positions. They could also join the priests and serve the Zapotec gods. It is certainly a different image of life than the members of many of the other civilizations at the time had because it seemed to offer a lot more freedom of movement within the commoner class. The noble class seemed to have less freedom and mobility because a lower noble could not become king. However, a slave who earned freedom could become a wealthy merchant over time.

# At Home

The remnants of the different structures provide a look into the types of homes and buildings that were common. These structures were as impressive as the resident could make them. Their religious structures saw regular ceremonies and sacrifices as they tried to appease Sky and Earth, and beg for their ancestors to intercede during times of crisis and problems. Each village also had its own government building, although the type of governance that was conducted in them is largely left up to the imagination. There were also schools and dry-goods stores where education and commerce were conducted. Most villages even had a medical facility where the sick and wounded were tended to on a regular basis.

The average home was made of stone and mortar, and archeologists can still find them today. They were noticeably smaller than the homes of the nobles, but they were still adequate for the families who lived in them. Nobles required larger homes because the males typically had between 10 and 15 wives. With such a large family, they needed a much larger residence than a farmer who only had one wife. Outside of the noble class, the only men who were able to keep multiple wives were the men who were wealthy. This was often the merchants, although some of the innovators were also successful enough to have more than one wife.

# Early Astronomers and the Passage of Time

The Zapotecs were one of the first civilizations to look to the stars, which is not surprising given the fact that they believed they descended from the clouds. However, they did much more than just admire the stars. The Zapotecs created a calendar that was not too different from the European calendar, although they dealt with the extra days a little differently than the Europeans did.

Unlike the Europeans, the Zapotecs believed that time was part of a repetitive cycle. Instead of constantly progressing forward, time would return to the same point over the years, and it would move through the same cycle over and over again.

Like the European calendar, the Zapotec calendar based their timeline on their religion. According to their calendar, a year had 260 days and was divided into four months. Months were more closely aligned to the seasons because the Zapotec civilization was based on agriculture. The seasons of the year played a vital role in the activities and the decisions of the Zapotecs. Each month was 65 days long, and contained five weeks. Each week had 13 days. This calendar dictated the activities based on the rituals. The division of the calendar into four parts represented the movement of time in its repetitive cycle.

The Zapotecs had a second calendar that was based on the sun's cycles. This calendar was distinctly different from the ritual calendar, dividing the year into much finer sections to better plan for the agrarian needs based on the specific movements of the sun. Structuring their lives around a calendar that reflected this made it easier to track the needs of the farmers. This calendar had 18 months that were 20 days each. An additional five days were added to the year to keep the calendar current with the seasons. This offered a more regular structure to their months instead of varying the number of days in each month.

It is interesting to note that many of the artifacts and relics found in the Zapotec ruins include the names of the people whose remains were discovered. Archeologists have noted that the Zapotecs tended to name their children after the days of the calendar, and it is believed that the name reflects the day the child was born. The Zapotecs believed in luck, and certain days were considered lucky. Children of the members of the nobility tended to be named after the lucky days closest to when they were born instead of being named for the day they were born. It was common that the remains of nobles would have names like "9 Flower" or "8 Deer" to reflect their place in society as well as providing a rough estimate of when they were born. They also received nicknames that reflected days, although it is difficult to say where those nicknames originated. Men were often nicknamed "Lightning Creator" or "Great Eagle" and the names may have stemmed from accomplishments or close ties to the ruler.

# Bumper Crop

Maize, or corn as it is also known, was an early favorite crop of the Zapotecs as it provided the greatest return for the least amount of work. Not that maize was easy to farm, but it was far simpler and more stable than other crops that were grown in the early days. The Zapotecs continued to grow other foods, but maize was the staple on which their culture relied to sustain itself.

Outside of Monte Albán, the land was largely fertile and very conducive to regular bumper crops to support the growing civilization. It was an ideal place to grow maize without having to spend as much time defending their work from neighbors because they were more removed from those warlike neighbors. This played a large role in the civilization's ability to grow and thrive. Without maize, it would have been far more difficult for the Zapotecs to have established such a large and cultured nation that helped to change the mentality and path of the peoples in Mesoamerica.

It is perhaps ironic that while the Zapotecs relied on the crop and those who farmed it, farmers were not as highly regarded as the leaders and the priests who served largely auxiliary functions. Without the farmers and their regular production of maize, there would not have been a Zapotec nation.

# Other Crops and Food

Maize was the most important crop, but it was far from the only one that the Zapotecs grew. Although the capital was located in an arid place, many places within the empire offered ideal conditions for growing many different crops. There were three distinct types of soil and regions for farming, and various types of agriculture were practiced based on the type of irrigation required to sustain the plants. The ability to innovate and develop the various methods of farming was a large part of the reason for the ability of the Zapotecs to survive.

1. The lands in and around Monte Albán were stony. However, evaporation was slower than in some other areas.

2. The land in the valley was much richer and better for growing crops. The evaporation rate was much faster than it was in the mountains.

3. The Piedmont area was the most varied as it sloped and dipped, making the land more difficult to till, but easier to ensure the water required was available.

Tailoring the agricultural needs to the specific region, the Zapotec had five distinctive methods of farming.

1. Rainfall farming was carried out in areas where rain was common and plentiful. These areas required less robust irrigation and had more reliable crop growth.

2. Well irrigation was required for areas where the water was further underground.

3. Canal irrigation was used to provide water to areas where rain and water were less frequent. This was one of the most advanced types of supplying water to those areas.

4. Floodwater farming was used in areas where there was a lot of water, but the rain tended to be dumped all at once.

5. Hillside terracing provided a way of delivering water to piedmont areas and higher regions where water was more difficult to find.

Different plants were planted and harvested across the regions depending on the needs of the crops. In addition to maize, the Zapotecs relied on beans, avocados, tomatoes, squash, chili peppers, prickly pear cactuses, and agaves to keep their people fed. There were also special foods grown for the nobility, such as cocoa beans for chocolate.

In addition to farming, they continued to forage for foods like herbs and acorns. Although dogs were raised for food, hunting was prevalent. Large game was restricted to the noble class, but there were plenty of other small game animals that commoners could eat, including turtles, gophers, lizards, and doves. Although commoners were not allowed to eat the bigger game, they frequently hunted with the nobles. This helped to bring the community together as they worked toward a common goal.

## The Role of Tributes

The Zapotecs tended to expand through peaceful means, but there were times when they extended their borders through war. When they conquered a people who were not willing to join them peacefully, the people of the defeated areas were required to pay tribute to the conquering Zapotecs. This reminded them that they were part of a new culture. The leaders of larger regions operated the military and provided the necessary support as determined by the king.

The only regular members of this military were the noblemen who were assigned to a particular position. The commoners required to do most of the fighting were called to serve as needed. Soldiers who distinguished themselves in battle were rewarded with special outfits and indicators that marked them as being superior to the average fighter.

Although this type of military proved to be more advanced than that of their neighbors and the their fortifications provided much better protection from invaders, the Zapotecs were still inclined to settle disputes through diplomacy whenever possible. The method used by the Zapotecs to command and fill the military ranks and the use of diplomacy were also innovations that they used to their advantage.

# Chapter 7 – The Arts, Athletics, and Technology

Perhaps one of the fascinating things about the Zapotecs was how much more advanced they were in terms of the arts and sports. Writing began early in their civilization and continued to play a crucial role over the course of the empire's existence. Their language was intricate, and that was reflected in the hieroglyphs they used to express themselves. Zapotec artisans created delicate works of jewelry and pottery that helped to distinguish which works were from their society and which artifacts belonged to other nations. They were also excellent sportsmen, and there were times when those sports were played with neighboring civilizations.

## A Highly Developed Language

One of the most notable aspects of the Zapotecs was their language. It was part of the ancient Mesoamerican family group called Oto-Manguean. When different people who used the Oto-Manguean language began to splinter and scatter around 1,500 BC, the Zapotecs were quick to change the language to meet their own needs. The meaning of words was reflected in the tone used when the word was spoken. Languages today like Italian and Spanish are tonal as well, with the tone of the speaker's voice being an indication of what is meant.

Although it is impossible to know exactly how the language sounded in the early phases of the empire, Zapotec is still spoken in parts of Mexico today, including the areas around Northern and Southern Sierra, the Central Valleys, and the Isthmus of Tehuantepec. Although it has certainly changed since the peak of the civilization, there are hints of how the language was used during the time of the Zapotecs.

# The Intricacies of the Written Word

The Zapotecs were among the first to begin recording information in the region. Their writing system would be mimicked by the other major cultures in Mesoamerica, including the Mayans, the Mixtecs, and the Aztecs. Most of the writing told stories about their conquests and leaders. Some of the remaining artifacts tell stories that would have otherwise been lost to time, although the stories are usually fragmented and incomplete.

Their writing was similar to the Ancient Egyptians as stories were told in pictures that told a story based on the positioning of the figure. The writing was logo syllabic, meaning that a symbol was dedicated to each syllable of the words they spoke. Reading was more akin to the eastern tradition, reading columns of text from top to bottom instead of left to right. Despite what archaeologists have been able to decipher of their writing, there is still much that remains a mystery because the language is so complicated.

Writing appeared during the early days of the civilization, and much of it focused on the vanquishing of enemies. The leader of San José Mogote had art made that depicted him conquering his enemies and sacrificing them to show his dominance and superiority. It is currently the oldest instance of Zapotec writing, but it is not a surprise that it was used to indicate the successes of the ruler. Given that the people were always struggling against their neighbors, this would have been something everyone knew was necessary to ensure their survival. By focusing on competition and being successful in their struggles, the Zapotecs were validating their abilities and the superiority of their gods. Many works in early human writing reflect a similar struggle and overcoming of others.

One of the primary locations where archeologists have encountered writing is among the burial places of the dead. The Zapotecs buried their people with items that spoke of who they were. The writing reflects their station and accomplishments that are still being deciphered by archeologists. Writing appeared to be used primarily as a way of recording genealogical information by the time the civilization was thriving in the Valley of Oaxaca. This was quite a shift from the early days when it was primarily used to show dominance and justify the deeds of Zapotec leaders. Inscriptions have been found at all known burial sites from the time the Zapotec civilization was established. Unlike today, writing was a way of recording history so it would not be forgotten, and not as a source of entertainment or news. However, the inscriptions do tell elaborate tales that are probably enhancements of the facts.

Many remains are also marked with writings that tell stories and details about what the objects were used for. In the case of tombs, the writing tells stories of the accomplishments and history of the people buried within them. Powerful animals were used to represent powerful rulers, with big cats being one of the most popular representations. Flying animals were used to represent other members of the noble family who would one day return to the skies in the form of clouds. Warriors were denoted by the use of dangerous predators that were not used to represent the king.

The Zapotecs believed speech was different between the two classes. Over time, they came to have different speech patterns and images. Members of the nobility were thought to have a more elegant manner of speech, and commoners were considered to have speech that was filled with lies and inaccuracies. Although it is unlikely that the speech was significantly different, it was undoubtedly portrayed differently in writing. Nobles were written about using more elegant scrawling language. It is the language of the nobility that is represented today in the various edifices and structures that remain. This was likely due in part to the possibility that the leaders were using the speech as propaganda for their people. By showing themselves as stronger and more honest, the nobles would be kept in awe by the commoners.

## Intricate Artifacts

Among their many accomplishments, the Zapotecs were experts at working with gold and silver to make amazing pieces of jewelry. They could make incredibly detailed designs and embellished larger pieces, resulting in some of the most artistic pieces in Mesoamerica. Many of these pieces were given to the rulers, and it was an honor for an artist when a ruler wore a particular piece of an artist's work.

Jade was used exclusively for the nobles, and it was added to many of their accessories. From their ear ornaments to decorations placed in their lips, jade highlighted the place in society that someone held. It was one of the few precious minerals that was used by the Zapotecs. Remains of the Zapotecs who have jade ornaments make it easier to identify them as important people within their communities.

Much of what archaeologists have learned about the Zapotecs is through examining their pottery. While pots and ceramics had functional purposes, such as storing water, eating, and during ceremonies, they also played a role in burials and decoration of homes. Doubling as a tool and a symbol, pottery provides some insight into the lives of the Zapotecs. The pots and ceramics that were functional were usually worn and largely undecorated. Other pots and ceramics were very detailed, telling a story or providing an aesthetically pleasing appearance. Most of the people discovered in the Zapotec regions were buried with pots, which they could use in the afterlife. The more intricate the pot, usually the higher the status of the person with whom it was buried.

# A Healthy Sense of Competition

As a people who preferred diplomacy to fighting, the Zapotecs tended to hold friendly competitions with their neighbors. During Monte Albán phase 2, ball courts became common. The ball courts look similar to the shape of the Roman numeral for one (I), and it was a place for the Zapotecs to play and exercise. The game itself has been lost to time; even the descendants of the Zapotecs do not know how the ball game was played or what the rules were.

Based on the number of ball courts in the cities and villages, it is clear that it was one of the favorite pastimes of the people, perhaps like soccer is today. Some places have large rectangular areas that archeologists assume were used for the sport because there are no other locations that could have be used for playing the game. Looking over the hieroglyphs at the courts, it appears the game required participants to wear knee guards, gloves, and other protective gear as they played the sport. The ball was made from the rubber tree, giving it more bounce than if it had been made of animal skin or other materials.

The city of Dainzu has the most famous ball court. Located at the base of an easily defensible hill, it was the ideal location to play sports. Since the location was easy to protect, it was difficult for enemies to sneak up on the Zapotecs while they were relaxing and playing. On the lowest terrace of the Dainzu complex are carved walls that display details not of slain enemies, but of competitors in the sport. It is an intricately carved wall that is unlike anything else in the Zapotec ruins, and it has captured the attention and imagination of many who have seen it. The ball court is not shaped like many of the other courts. The court that has been most studied is rectangular in shape instead of being shaped like the Roman numeral I. However, there is another ball court in Dainzu that does conform to the type of court found in the capitals of the Zapotecs. The writing on the first ball court provides just enough details to encourage archeologists to make guesses about the game. However, there is not enough information or detail to help archaeologists to ever be fully confident they know how the sport was played or exactly what its role was in the Zapotec society. They are continually revising their ideas of the game based on the latest findings.

# A Look into Technology's Roots

The Zapotecs were able to turn an arid, apparently uninhabitable mountain into their thriving capital city of Monte Albán, and proved that they were more advanced and logical than many of the other civilizations around them. They were able to adapt and build their environment to suit their needs instead of learning to work within the limitations of a particular area.

Easily one of their greatest accomplishments, the Zapotecs were able to grow their civilization and thrive in areas where other civilizations could not because they had their own form of irrigation. Using a series of canals, they could ensure that water was free-flowing and available regardless of the limited amount of rainfall that fell in the region.

One of the main sources of water came from the Atoyac River, the river that flowed through the Valley of Oaxaca. It provided the water needed to sustain the crops and population when there was no rain. From this river and small streams that fed into it, the Zapotecs created irrigation systems and directed the water up to higher regions. This meant the water was distributed without taking any away from the crops. There is also evidence they created a dam to increase and store a large amount of water where it was needed.

Architecture in the Zapotec civilization was also different from many of their neighbors. While they also built pyramids, many of the remaining structures appear similar to the kinds of structures found in Europe at the time. For example, the most studied ball court in Dainzu had intricately designed walls. The more common types of ball courts were lined with stands that were probably for the spectators to watch the game. Looking at these remains calls to mind bleachers and stages where people could sit to be entertained.

However, it is the burials that have the most intriguing architecture. The dead were buried underground in tombs, regardless of the station and class of the deceased. These tombs were located below the floors of the homes where they lived. Stairs led down from the home into the vestibule outside of the tomb. It is probable that this was symbolic of the passing from this world into the next. Though only the members of the noble class had ancestors who could intercede, commoners still held their ancestors in reverence, as is made clear by the structures where the dead are buried. The tombs also had intricate designs and decorations added to them to tell the stories of the dead.

# Chapter 8 – Two Worlds Collide

The Zapotecs had been a well-established civilization long before the arrival of the Conquistadors. The capital that had been the center of their growth for centuries was already in decline and was no longer the center of arts and innovation. There were clear signs the civilization was in decline, both because of internal and external forces.

While there is no way to know what the internal politics were at the time of the arrival of the Spanish, it was a civilization that was apparently past its peak. The transfer of power from Monte Albán to the religious center of Milta was a sign that things were shifting. Had the Conquistadors not invaded, it is possible that an entirely new civilization would have risen from the decay. However, this was a period in Mesoamerican history where an outside force altered the trajectory.

## The End of a War

The Zapotecs had warred with the Aztecs for nearly a year before the arrival of the Conquistadors. The Zapotecs had not been the victors. Given the way they had dominated their neighbors for so long, or found diplomatic solutions to power struggles, the battle with the Aztecs must have taken a much harsher toll on the aging Zapotec civilization. It is not certain exactly what happened or how the Aztecs had won the war. The Aztecs were at the peak of their civilization, and they dominated their area. Had the Conquistadors not arrived, it is possible they would have ended up incorporating the Zapotecs into the Aztec Empire.

Innovation and new ideas had become less frequent, and they had not undergone any substantial changes in several hundred years. The Aztecs were more warlike than the Zapotecs, so it is probable that the growing nation would have wholly consumed the Zapotecs into their society.

Before the Conquistadors arrived, a war ended with minimal loss to the Zapotecs. Although the war had been longer and bloodier than the Zapotecs were accustomed to, they had negotiated favorable terms with the Aztecs. With the king of the Zapotecs accepting a bride from the Aztecs, annual tributes to the Aztecs, and small Aztec garrisons within the realm of the Zapotecs, it appears that the shift of power towards the Aztecs was in progress. If not for the interference of the Europeans at this point, the civilization of the Zapotecs may have been long lost to time. It is possible their extensive history would have been all but wiped out by the Aztecs.

There is no way to know how the strained relationship would have worked out had it taken its natural course. What is known is that the relationship between the Aztecs and Zapotecs was not ideal for the future of the Zapotec civilization.

# The Conquistadors' Arrival

The Conquistadors arrived before the Zapotecs had disappeared and their existence was of interest to the Spanish. Having been around far longer than the Aztecs, the Zapotecs had a much more structured society; one that was familiar to the Spanish. They could draw comparisons between the aging empire and their own experiences, something that was difficult to do with the Aztecs.

Although the arrival of the Conquistadors resulted in a record of the existence of the Zapotecs and kept the civilization from disappearing into oblivion, there is no doubt that the arrival of the Spanish also signaled the end of the declining civilization.

Hernán Cortés arrived in Mexico in the early 1500s, soon after the end of the war between the Zapotec and Aztec Empires. This mission was one that he had set out for himself and one that he was ordered by his superior, the governor of Cuba, not to begin. Initially, Cortés was interested in taking over the Aztec empire. Cortés operated in a way that was very opportunistic. By making friends with the enemies of the Aztecs, and eliminating some of the their allies, Cortés was able to maneuver his men into a better position, both physically and militarily. He succeeded in taking over the Aztec capital, but he soon left when he heard that the Spanish were coming to arrest him since he had followed through with a mission they had specifically ordered him not to undertake.

Following the conquering of the Aztecs, the Zapotecs were hopeful it would mean a return to their original way of life. Without the Aztecs dominating the region, this seemed possible, although the threat of the Conquistadors should also have been clear at that point. The Spanish were more interested in dominating and forcing their way of life on the people, claiming the land for their country. The warning signs were there, but the Zapotecs were more optimistic. That was probably because no one in Mesoamerica had ever seen anything quite like the Conquistadors before their arrival.

# A Tentative Peace

The Spanish were very interested in learning more about the Zapotecs, and they probably realized just how different the Zapotec outlook on life was compared to the other natives they had encountered. The Zapotec society was far more familiar than dissimilar to the one that the Spanish knew. While they viewed the cannibalism and sacrificing of humans to the gods as barbaric, even this was not too different compared to the history of Spain. The Spanish Inquisition was still prevalent in Spain at the time that the

Conquistadors were invading the civilizations in Mesoamerica. This meant they were not entirely unsympathetic to the idea of sacrificing humans for a religious cause. It was perhaps hypocritical they viewed the Zapotec sacrificial rituals as barbaric without condemning the violence and atrocities that were occurring in Spain at that time.

Whatever their personal feelings were about the Zapotecs, it was certain that the Spanish Conquistadors were impressed by the organization of the society and religion. This is evident from the way that they frequently compare the Zapotecs to their own royal lines and the Roman Catholic Church in their writings.

The Conquistadors began to ask questions of the Zapotecs. The interrogations were meant as a way of gathering information and learning about the natives of the land they would eventually conquer (although they may not have been aware of that at the time). The Spanish had two periods when they questioned the Zapotecs, in 1578 and 1581. The reflections of the people that they questioned offer a glimpse into the way the Zapotecs viewed themselves, even if the information was a little skewed by the lack of full understanding of the information the Zapotecs were trying to impart. Much of the information that was provided has been studied and learned by archeologists as a starting point for better understanding the ruins and artifacts that they encounter at archeological sites. Of course, skepticism should be employed when reading the writings as they are not perfect representations of the lives of the Zapotecs. However, it does provide valuable information about these people since archeologists are still working to unravel the meanings of most of the hieroglyphs left by the once great civilization.

The Conquistadors questioned the Zapotec king, Cociyopii, the last ruler of his dynasty. They inquired about his "idolatrous" religion and their practices. Later, he would be baptized and renamed Don Juan Cortés. The way the Spanish understood, or perhaps misunderstood, the ideas and descriptions that Cociyopii relayed created nearly as many questions as they resolved: however, the imperfect records do provide details that would likely have been lost to time had the Spanish not attempted to understand and write about the Zapotecs.

There is no way to know exactly how many people were living in the Zapotec nation when the Conquistadors arrived. The borders of the different civilizations changed often, and the Mesoamericans did not take a census of how many people there were in their empires. At the time, the Zapotecs still ruled over a large area, well beyond the Valley of Oaxaca.

# The Fall of an Empire

One of the few things on which archeologists can agree about the fall of the empire is that it happened after the arrival of the Conquistadors. There are different theories on what caused the decline. The diseases brought by the Spanish took a significant toll on the Zapotecs, just as European diseases negatively affected natives in North and South America. Given the size of the Zapotec empire, it is inconceivable that disease wiped out the entire nation. However, the diseases probably did cause serious problems for the areas that were more populous because there may not have been enough people left to continue with vital functions within the society, such as food production.

Despite the initial hope following the fall of the Aztec empire, the Zapotecs did not fare any better under the rule of the Conquistadors. They had a proud heritage and religion that were completely contrary to the government and religion the Spanish forced on every nation they conquered. Although the last ruler did give in and allow himself to be baptized into the Christian religion, this was more likely a sign that the nation would not survive the invasion, even if illness had not devastated the people from the different regions.

After this, the nation began to break apart much more rapidly. With the loss and conversion of the king from the religion they had practiced for more than 1,000 years, many villages and regions probably saw this as their opportunity to become autonomous. Some historians and archaeologists believe the empire fell to infighting as different pieces broke away to rule themselves. It would have become impossible for the nation to re-emerge after losing so many areas that had been crucial to maintaining the kind of social structure they had before that period. Also, the loss of the king would have been a serious blow to their religion. If he was the descendant of the gods and he chose to turn away from them that meant the people of the civilization no longer had the foundation for the hierarchical society that had dominated their lives. The loss of their religion would have been a significant blow to the whole civilization. Without their religion, chiefs and other leaders would have seen an opportunity to gain power they could not have held under the king. Commoners may also have seen a chance to reach well above their station.

Mitla continued to be a center for the remaining Zapotecs who clung to their old way of life. They continued to live and work there, even after the Conquistadors conquered their nation.

However, many of the former Zapotec people moved on and started new lives under a new structure. Some of them disappeared, either being added to other cultures or trying to live in areas where they could not survive. Some moved on and created little pockets that kept some of the ways of their ancestors. These people survived through the centuries and still speak a dialect that is descended from the Zapotec language. Some of the knowledge of their ancestors has been recorded, but much of it has been lost. Myths and stories have survived, but they have changed over time, so they do not entirely align with the recordings of the Conquistadors. They are the only link to a people who once ruled a large portion of Mesoamerica. When most of the rest of the world around them sought to force ideas and beliefs on their neighbors, the Zapotecs offered other solutions that meant entirely avoiding war when possible. With their ever-growing reach, many of the smaller civilizations saw an opportunity for a better life by joining the Zapotec people. The fact that the Zapotecs were adept at war was another reason to join them peacefully. They were one of the few civilizations in the area who sought other means of expanding, and their influence is impossible to overstate for the region.

# Conclusion

The Zapotec civilization was one of the earliest and most influential civilizations in Mesoamerica. While many budding civilizations looked to expand through conquering, the Zapotecs were more interested in innovation and technology. Their first capital in San José Mogote shows many of the early hallmarks of the civilization they would become. As their neighbors focused on resources and growth, the Zapotecs were beginning to form their own language and writing. The hieroglyphs they used during this time were later changed and incorporated into more intricate works. Even before they left San José Mogote, the Zapotecs demonstrated a much different interest in the world around them. They revered the food they killed because it contained a spirit from the gods, and sought to find balance with their world. It was this interest that ultimately led to the founding of a completely unique civilization in Mesoamerica.

When resources were scarce and constant battles began to wear on the Zapotecs, they moved. Opting to take a less traditional and easy path, the Zapotecs moved to an area that others had avoided. Leveling the top of a mountain for a new city, they began to build an empire that would be unlike any other in the region for several hundred years. They created irrigation systems that allowed them to live in dry areas where no other people would settle. Because of their innovation and intelligence, they established themselves in areas that were much easier to defend from other, warlike nations. The new city at Monte Albán was heavily fortified in addition to being difficult to reach. This ensured the population could pursue other interest rather than having to focus on war.

The Zapotec civilization found its footing and established itself as a people more interested in diplomacy than war for their early days. Even after they began to expand beyond their early boundaries, the Zapotecs tended to pursue peaceful resolutions. However, when forced to fight, they proved to be adept at waging war.

The people living within this ancient Mesoamerican civilization were free to live their lives in a way that was largely unfamiliar in Europe where slaves were usually slaves for the rest of their lives and the classes were rigidly defined into subsets. While the society was strictly divided between those who were believed to be descended from their gods and everyone else, the commoners were not limited in their potential as long as they did not aspire to marry members of the nobility or hold positions of power. Commoners could pursue their interests and abilities to add to the reputation of the Zapotecs. There were many positions within the nation as well. Farming was one of the primary jobs, but within cities and large villages, there was a wealth of artists and innovators who made beautiful and intricate works that established these people as being among the most refined for their time.

With a history that was over 1,000 years long and a way of thinking that was dissimilar to many of their neighbors at the time, the Zapotecs will always provide a completely new perspective for archaeologists and historians to explore.

# Check out another book by Captivating History

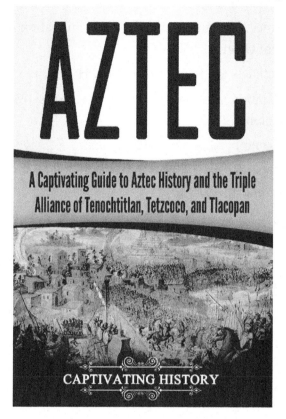

# Bibliography

Hernán Cortés Biography, Biography.com,

The Lost Zapotec: Vibrant Mesoamerican Civilization of the Cloud People, Ancient Origins, 2013-201.

These Zapotec Facts are Really Intriguing, Historyplex, 2018.

Zapotec Civilization, Ancient History Encyclopedia, Mark Cartwright, October 28, 2013.

Zapotec Civilization, Maya Inca Aztec, 2017.

Zapotec Civilization: A Civilization of the "Cloud People," Ancient Civilizations, June 18, 2016.

Zapotec Digs in Mexico Show Clues to Rise and Fall, National Graphic News, John Roach, March 9, 2009.

https://study.com/academy/lesson/why-is-monte-alban-historically-important.html - Image

# Free Bonus from Captivating History (Available for a Limited time)

Hi History Lovers!

Now you have a chance to join our exclusive history list so you can get your first history ebook for free as well as discounts and a potential to get more history books for free! Simply visit the link below to join.

Captivatinghistory.com/ebook

Also, make sure to follow us on:

Twitter: @Captivhistory

Facebook: Captivating History: @captivatinghistory

# ABOUT CAPTIVATING HISTORY

A lot of history books just contain dry facts that will eventually bore the reader. That's why Captivating History was created. Now you can enjoy history books that will mesmerize you. But be careful though, hours can fly by, and before you know it; you're up reading way past bedtime.

Get your first history book for free here:
http://www.captivatinghistory.com/ebook

Make sure to follow us on Twitter: @CaptivHistory
and Facebook: www.facebook.com/captivatinghistory so you can get all of our updates!

Made in the USA
Coppell, TX
31 October 2020